Eating Strong

By Vikki McIntyre

Illustrated by Mila Aydingoz

We respect and honour Aboriginal and Torres Strait Islander Elders past, present and future. We acknowledge the stories, traditions and living cultures of Aboriginal and Torres Strait Islander peoples on this land and commit to building a brighter future together.

Library For All Ltd.

Our ancestors knew how to eat strong

Long before supermarkets, our ancestors knew exactly how to eat strong. They lived healthy lives, eating food found on Country and in the sea. Good nutrition kept their bodies strong and their minds sharp.

But, over time, our way of eating has changed a lot. Understanding these changes can help us make better choices today and bring back strong eating habits.

Culture adapts over time, and now we mix traditional ways of eating with introduced ways.

Nutrition before colonisation

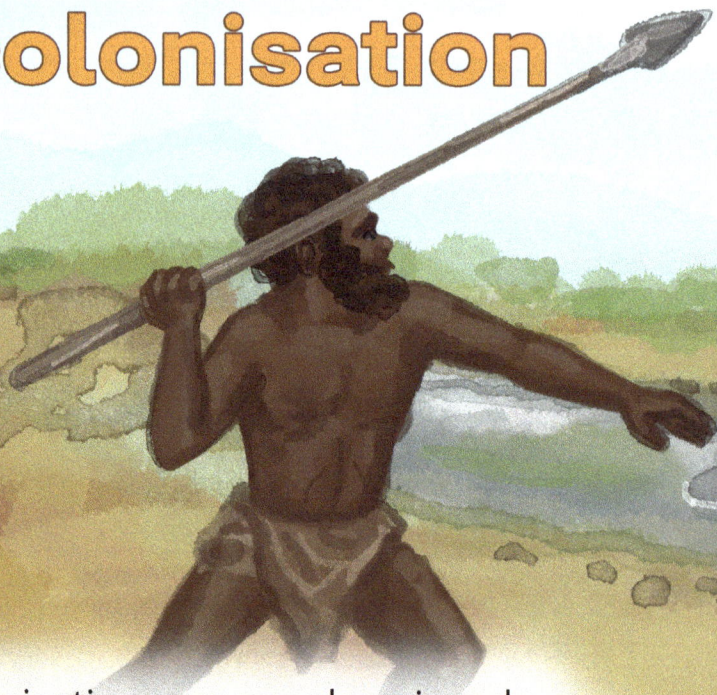

Before colonisation, our people enjoyed a balanced diet straight from Country. Families hunted kangaroos, emus, and fish, and gathered yams, berries, nuts, seeds, and greens. Food like turtle, dugong, and other seafood nourished us. This food gave us all the nutrition we needed for strength, growth, and energy.

Traditional diets had lots of protein from meat and fish, vitamins from fruit and vegetables, and healthy fats from nuts and seeds. Communities shared knowledge about what to eat, where to find food, and how to cook it safely and respectfully. This knowledge closely connected people to the land and each other.

Changes since colonisation

Colonisation brought new food like flour, sugar, tea, and canned goods. At first, this food seemed easy and tasty, but it soon replaced healthy, traditional food. Today, many of us rely on food high in sugar, salt, and unhealthy fats. This has led to health problems like diabetes, heart disease, and obesity.

Over time, losing access to traditional lands, along with the cost of food and its availability, has made healthy eating harder. Fast food and processed snacks (food changed from its natural state by cooking, preserving, or packaging) are quick and easy. But they don't nourish our bodies the way fresh food from Country does.

What does good nutrition look like?

Good nutrition means eating lots of different food to give our bodies energy and strength, and protect us from getting sick.

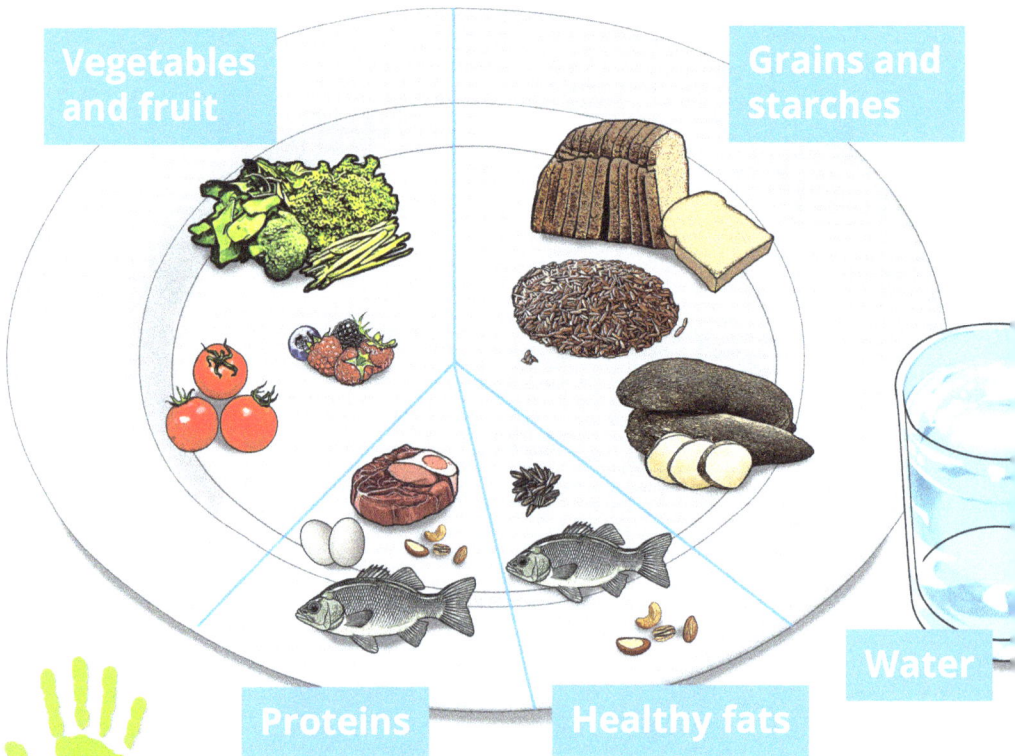

Vegetables and fruit

Grains and starches

Proteins

Healthy fats

Water

Here's a simple table showing what good nutrition looks like and why it's important.

Food group	Examples	Why it's important
Proteins	Kangaroo, fish, eggs, nuts	Helps build muscles and grow strong bodies
Vegetables and fruit	Bush tomatoes, berries, leafy greens	Boosts immunity and keeps organs healthy
Grains and starches	Yams, wholegrain bread, brown rice	Gives lasting energy
Healthy fats	Nuts, seeds, fish	Supports brain function and heart health
Water	Fresh, clean water	Keeps bodies hydrated and working well

Healthy eating guide

Here is a simple guide showing what food to eat and how many serves to aim for each day.

Food group	Serves per day	Serving size examples
Proteins	2–3 serves	100g meat or fish
		2 eggs
		handful of nuts
Vegetables and fruit	5 serves	1 cup leafy greens
		medium-sized fruits
		handful of berries
Grains and starches	3–6 serves	1 slice wholegrain bread
		½ cup cooked rice
Healthy fats	1–2 serves	small handful of nuts
		tablespoon of seeds
Water	6–8 glasses	250ml glass of water

Each food group can be represented by a variety of pictures, icons, or symbols. Here are some examples.

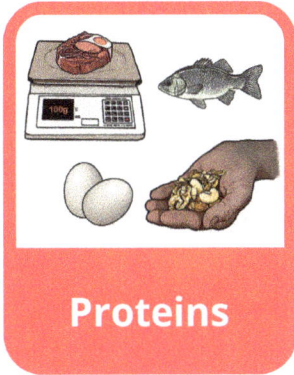

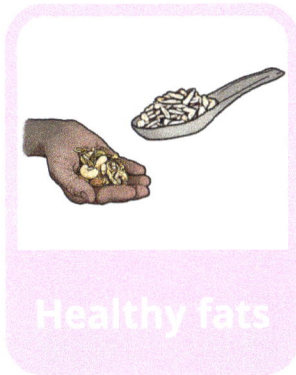

Proteins

Vegetables and fruit

Grains and starches

Healthy fats

Water

Bringing traditional food back

Kangaroo and emu meat are lean and full of protein and nutrients. This makes them healthier choices than processed meat. Fish and seafood provide good nutrition, especially in our communities on the islands or near the coast. Eating this food regularly helps keep us strong and healthy, just like our ancestors.

Kangaroo meat

Fish and seafood

Bush tomato

Kakadu plum

Wattleseed

Lemon myrtle

Our traditional bush food is still very healthy and good for us today. We can easily use bush tomato, Kakadu plum, wattleseed, and lemon myrtle in our meals. Eating this food connects us back to culture and keeps traditional knowledge alive.

Impact of introduced food

Food like sugar, flour, and processed products has had a big impact on our people's health. Processed food often contains extra sugar, salt, and preservatives. Refined food, like white flour, has had important nutrients removed during processing. This food often doesn't have the nutrients we need and can lead to health problems when we eat it too often.

Sugar is not so sweet

Sugar can cause diabetes and tooth decay, while processed flour and refined grains add to obesity and heart disease.

Eating less of this introduced food and eating more traditional and fresh food helps us stay healthier. Choosing whole foods over processed snacks is a great step towards better nutrition.

Eating strong today

We can honour our ancestors by eating more traditional food and being aware of the food introduced by colonisation. Learning about nutrition helps us make better choices and stay connected to culture. We can live healthier, happier lives.

Next time you're choosing what to eat, think about the strong, nutritious food your ancestors relied on. Eating strong today means respecting the past, caring for our bodies, and looking forward to healthier futures.

Photo Credits

Page	Attribution
Page 12 (bush tomato)	Mark Marathon/commons.wikimedia.org
Page 12 (Kakadu plum)	Leanne Atheron/Austockphoto.com.au
Page 12 (wattleseed)	CSIRO/commons.wikimedia.org
Page 12 (lemon myrtle)	lynnebeclu/istockphoto.com
Page 12 (kangaroo meat)	EddWestmacott/istockphoto.com
Page 12 (fish and seafood)	garten-gg/pixabay.com
Pages 14–15	Mukhina1/istockphoto.com

You can use these questions to talk about this book with your family, friends and teachers.

What did you learn from this book?

Describe this book in one word. Funny? Scary? Colourful? Interesting?

How did this book make you feel when you finished reading it?

What was your favourite part of this book?

About the author

Vikki McIntyre was born in Sydney and grew up in the western suburbs. Her ancestral Country is the south coast of New South Wales. She descends from the saltwater people of the Dharawal language group. Vikki is happiest when she can feel sand under her feet and smell saltwater in the air.

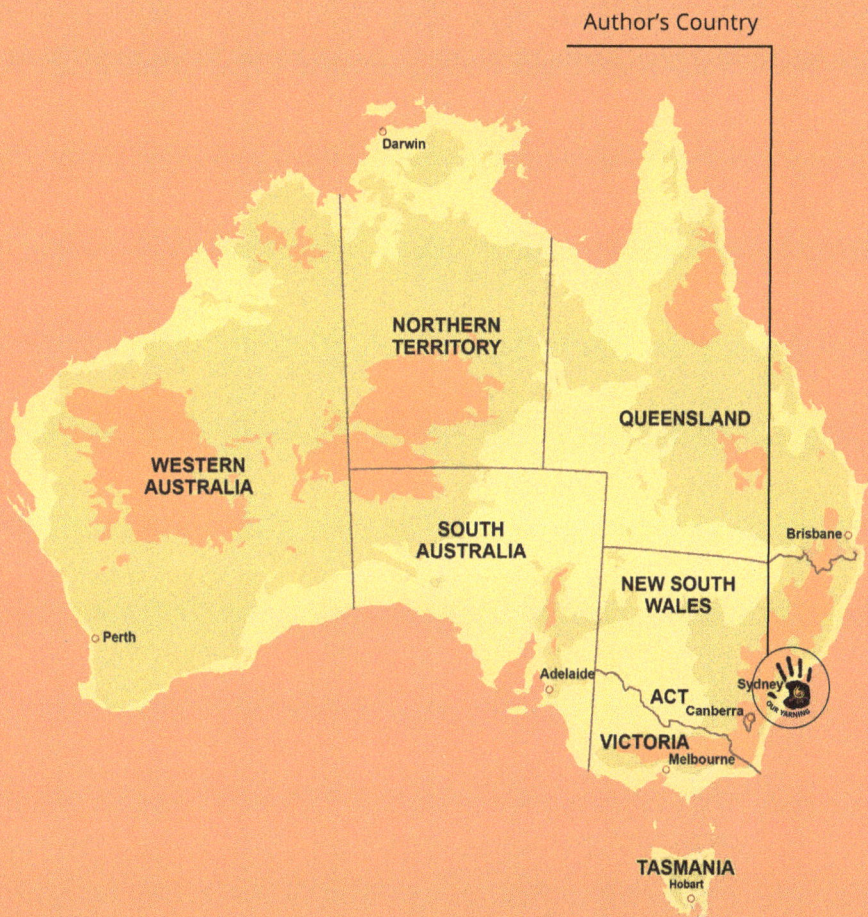

Author's Country

Darwin

NORTHERN
TERRITORY

QUEENSLAND

WESTERN
AUSTRALIA

SOUTH
AUSTRALIA

NEW SOUTH
WALES

Brisbane

Perth

Adelaide

Sydney

ACT
Canberra

VICTORIA
Melbourne

TASMANIA
Hobart

Our Yarning

The Our Yarning collection aligns with the Australian Curriculum through the Cross-Curriculum Priorities — Aboriginal and Torres Strait Islander Histories and Cultures. The collection provides an authentic opportunity for learning and embedding Aboriginal and Torres Strait Islander perspectives because it is written by Aboriginal and Torres Strait Islander people.

We know that children learn better, and enjoy reading more, when they see themselves in the stories, characters and illustrations of the books they read.

To download the app, visit the Google Play Store or Apple Store and search 'Our Yarning'.

libraryforall.org

You're reading Upper Primary

Learner – Beginner readers

Start your reading journey with short words, big ideas and plenty of pictures.

Level 1 – Rising readers

Raise your reading level with more words, simple sentences and exciting images.

Level 2 – Eager readers

Enjoy your reading time with familiar words, but complex sentences.

Level 3 – Progressing readers

Develop your reading skills with creative stories and some challenging vocabulary.

Level 4 – Fluent readers

Step up your reading skills with playful narratives, new words and fun facts.

Middle Primary – Curious readers

Discover your world through science and stories.

Upper Primary – Adventurous readers

Explore your world through science and stories.

Library For All is an Australian not for profit organisation with a mission to make knowledge accessible to all via an innovative digital library solution. Visit us at libraryforall.org

Eating Strong

First published 2025

Published by Library For All Ltd
Email: info@libraryforall.org
URL: libraryforall.org

This book was made possible by the generous contributions of GSK.

Our Yarning logo design by Jason Lee, Bidjipidji Art

Original illustrations by Mila Aydingoz

Eating Strong
McIntyre, Vikki
ISBN: 978-1-923554-92-4
SKU04958

www.ingramcontent.com/pod-product-compliance
Lightning Source LLC
Chambersburg PA
CBHW042343040426
42448CB00019B/3394